# The Reluctant Poet

By Vance Johnson

ISBN 978-0-9831887-9-7

# Table of Contents

# Introduction:

Vance Johnson is both author and subject of many of his poems. He began writing poems after reading Shakespeare. The Sonnets of Shakespeare appealed to him. He felt the romance in them would help his game! He memorized Sonnet #116. He had a great deal of success associated with this technique.

The year was 1968 and he was a freshman at Penn State University. It was a short jump from reading Shakespeare's sonnets to creating his own.  In 2007 he wrote a poem titled "Time". He now has writings dating back to 2003. The job he had working in the Operating Room, in Neurosurgical Service allowed many hours of just sitting. This is a collection of those poems and writings (impressions).

# Narrative for "Time"

As a Surgical Nurse I would work long

Hours in the Neuro-Surgical Service.

In the Operating Room as a Circulator for

That Service. I would use that time during

The long cases to write.

So! During those times I would write notes

That would later become Poems

# Time

The Minutes too numerous to mention

Ticking and sailing by

To lose a few to daydreams

Would not make you blink an eye

Hours! Now that is something real

Often dragging on

An unexplained void, on occasion

Or a cloudy vision til morn

What can said of a day?

That often Anticipated

Calendar filling segment that says

**"We made it"**

# Narrative for By What Name?

As far back as I can remember it has

Always been "Iva and Vance". We were

Born 8 months apart. Iva the oldest.

Throughout our youth we were joined

At the hip. Iva (Brownies/Girl Scouts),

Vance (Cub Scouts and Boy Scouts). Our

Grandmother made sure we went to Olin

Mills to document everything with photos.

It was my responsibility to accompany

Iva to piano lesions, choir rehearsal and

Any event outside the house.

So! To write this poem was a pleasure.

Thanks for everything Sis!!!

# By What Name?

What would I call someone like me?

Born the same

Our early tracks through life were always

Side by side

What name would i give to one like me?

With skin and face

At a glance some might think it me

The one who holds my place

We were rivals in some games

Striking blow for blow

And shoulder to shoulder in another frame

Two entities joined at the soul

Who would take my defense?

In my absence

And knows the same can be said of me

For thee

By what name are you known?

The knower of my secrets

The looker through the window of my life

Offering my regrets

Companions during life's journey

Matching step for step

Occupying similar space and time

There! When the other slips

Who is the one who cares so much?

For hers and others

The one who has love for such and such

And has Love for you

So! By what name is she called?

What label is her's?

Simple is my word for her

Sister! No, call her "Sis"

# Narrative for "We May Never Meet Again"

This poem was written in memory of my

Late Son, Vance Denairo Johnson. Because my

Son was lost to me at an early Age, I would

wonder if our paths would Cross again.

Sometime in space. Some Ripple that bends

back Time and once again Our souls will meet.

Or will the day of his passing be our last

time together. At that time my thoughts were

not on my drive home from

the Hospital. My thoughts were about my last

few weeks visiting with my Son in his

Hospital room. This time allowed us time

To improve our Father/Son relationship.

# We May Never Meet Again

Looking back to many yesterday's ago

When our universe was whole

I never thought to look ahead

To see there a missing soul.

Now I face this life as is

But will I see the face of His

Could it be no other time?

That Spirits touch, His hand and mine.

Denairo

# Narrative for "Candace

My Pre-teen Niece came to visit my Wife

And I. She was so cute. We did Disney

World and she was a joy.

This poem is dedicated to her, "Candace"

During her stay Candace became my

Sidekick. She was eager to go with me

wherever I went.

# Candace

Like sunshine glowing bright,

You gave sparkle to our day

You were the orange glow of sunlight,

That chased the fleeing night away.

Your radiant, consistent smile.

The questions and the questions.

While being just a child.

Your worth, so much more to mention.

As the twelfth egg makes a dozen

And the creamy icing on a cake

Make complete, what wasn't

These are the things you make.

You be the sugar of my CAN-DACE

And I will be your Uncle Vance.

# Narrative for Keeping Less

This poem is more Philosophy than

Romance.

In a relationship I would say that if you

Observe your Partner you can determine

Your effectiveness and influence on them.

I think when your Girl or Guy is Smiling. It is

A good sign. The giving in a relationship

can bring about these reactions.

Keeping less

In this very short poem the idea is that you

Want to see in your Partner's eyes: Joy and

a smile on their lips.

# Keeping Less

I yearn for your Happiness

As if it were my own

A Smile upon your Face

Brings warmth to my Heart

The look in your Eyes

Tells me how to Feel

Love is Sharing more of Yourself

And keeping less of who you are

# Narrative for Wrote of Love

This poem is an example of what

Shakespeare and I have in common:

LOVE

In Shakespeare's sonnet #118 he speaks

Of what Love is not. So my few lines are

Stating what I believe Love to be.

# Wrote of Love

If I were Shakespeare and he wrote of

Love. I would write of things I know. No

Question or thought thereof.

I will not compare thee to Summer's Day!

No!!

I would write in the Voice of Two

The Synchronized flow, a majestic waltz,

Me and you.

Some happy romp and twilight show.

# Narrative for Sister Carol

This poem is dedicated to my younger

Sister, Carol. She was so far behind me

In school that I did not know any of her

Friends. Carol has lived in a home marred

By death. In 1969, our mother and then my

Sister-in-law later. In spite of the tragedies

That surrounded her home, she always

Stood tall.

I was absent for these tragedies in her life.

Sister Carol

However, I say now "Please take my Hand".

# Sister Carol

Hey girl! Take my hand

The one who holds my heart

Sis, so sorry! Please take my hand

Still waters run deep, as you know.

Glad we made it to tomorrow!

Never you mind if I don't tell strangers

Passing by about my Love for you.

Another Love of my life. Perhaps at the

Top of the list.

A Sister's kiss. A Mom we miss. Carol

The one that we talk about, who is quick

With a smile and slow to anger.

Hey Girl! Take my hand.

# Narrative for The Gift of Life

In this poem we ask that age old question.

Why are we here?

Why did the Lord give us this gift of Life?

I favor the notion that

We are given this precious gift in hopes

That we would follow his Word and live out

The purpose of our existence and therefore

Enjoy this Gift of Life

# The Gift of Life

The gift of life

Is truly a gift to me.

For I have it, not by request

But because it was meant to be.


When I am happy

This life I say was good to receive

And when I am sad

I wonder why it was given to me.


The gifts I give

The gifts I give are meant to please

Not to hurt

Not to hurt the receiver, you see

Now, Maybe life is more

Than a gift which is given and received.

Maybe it is the opportunity

To be a part of things that be.

# Narrative for "Always my Valentine"

This is a simple verse saying, Always My

Sweet Valentine

# Always My Valentine

February 14th a special day

For Lovers all to say "I love you, I love you

And these words I say to you


For us, we need no Special Time

Our Love is always on the Line.

Day by day we show the Truth

That we are here is our Proof


So! Asked what I got

Always my Valentine


I'll say it was a lot

A Lover, a Wife, a real Sweetheart

One who always does her part

After all these years

You're still looking Fine

Always My Sweet Valentine

# Narrative for He Knows

No matter what the effort or

How strong the desire to Please

Anytime along the way.

Displeasure or Anger spoils the Man's

Desire to bring Joy and Happiness

To Him and Their Family.

# He Knows

She questions my Loyalty

Wondering if I belong only to Her

She thinks he must certainly see the

Luscious curves in front of us. Not Me!!

Well, what about when the whole Flock

Comes by and I divert my eyes

Does your imperfection reveal itself?

Do you allow your insecurity to ruin the

Day?

He Knows

He knows in his mind there exist some

Scales. Where as in her mind the Scales, if

Any, tips in her favor

And if anyone is to be Evaluated, it is him

If anyone is to keep it in Balance, it is him

Not her!! He Knows!